Original title:
The Art of Being Together

Copyright © 2024 Swan Charm
All rights reserved.

Author: Paulina Pähkel
ISBN HARDBACK: 978-9916-86-881-2
ISBN PAPERBACK: 978-9916-86-882-9
ISBN EBOOK: 978-9916-86-883-6

Threads that Bind

In quiet moments, we weave our dreams,
With strands of hope, and moonlit beams.
Each story shared brings us together,
A tapestry rich, through any weather.

Through trials faced and joys we find,
In every heart, a thread entwined.
A bond unbroken, strong and bright,
Together we stand, in endless light.

Echoes of Laughter

In every room, a joyful sound,
Where memories linger, love is found.
With every chuckle, a spark ignites,
Turning dull days into starry nights.

We gather close, the stories flow,
In gentle whispers, our spirits grow.
Echoes of laughter, sweet serenade,
In heart's embrace, our fears do fade.

Starlit Conversations

Under the sky, with stars aglow,
We share our secrets, soft and low.
Each twinkling light a guiding word,
In silences deep, our hearts are heard.

With dreams adorned in silver light,
We journey through the tranquil night.
In every pause, a connection feels,
A universe spun, a truth that heals.

Hand in Hand on This Journey

With every step, side by side,
We face the waves, the rising tide.
Through valleys deep and mountains high,
In unity strong, our spirits fly.

The road is long, but hearts align,
Together we dance, the stars define.
In laughter and tears, we'll find our way,
Hand in hand, come what may.

Hearts Bathed in Warmth

In the glow of twilight's embrace,
Laughter dances, a soft trace.
With every heartbeat, stories unfold,
In shared whispers, our love is told.

Fingers entwined, a gentle fight,
Guided by stars, our dreams take flight.
Each moment savored, like a sweet wine,
Together we flourish, two souls divine.

Weaving Moments into Memory

Threads of laughter, woven tight,
In the tapestry of day and night.
Each shared glance, a stitch of grace,
In the fabric of time, we find our place.

Colors fade, but love remains bright,
Knit by the warmth of shared sunlight.
Every heartbeat, a note in the song,
With you beside me, where I belong.

Ocean of Affection

Waves of feelings crash and rise,
A sea of trust beneath the skies.
In every tide, our hopes ignite,
Together we journey, day and night.

Shores may shift, yet we stand firm,
Finding solace in love's warm balm.
An endless depth, where souls unite,
In the ocean of affection, pure delight.

Seasons of Together

Spring's bloom whispers sweet and clear,
Summer dances with warmth, so dear.
Autumn's hues paint life anew,
Winter wraps us in love's pure view.

Through every season, side by side,
With open hearts, we take each stride.
Time may change, yet we remain,
In every cycle, love's refrain.

Ties That Bind

Threads of love weave through my soul,
Connecting hearts, making us whole.
In laughter and tears, we find our way,
Through every storm, come what may.

In whispered secrets, our stories blend,
A bond unbroken, we will defend.
Through time's embrace, hand in hand,
Together we rise, together we stand.

A Dance in Unison

In moonlit nights, we twirl and sway,
With every step, we lose our way.
The music swells, our spirits rise,
In this moment, the world defies.

With eyes closed tight, we feel the beat,
Every heartbeat, a steady heat.
Lost in rhythm, our souls align,
In this dance, your heart is mine.

Echoes of Laughter

In the quiet night, echoes ring,
Memories of joy, in laughter we sing.
Beneath the stars, we share our dreams,
In every giggle, the moonlight beams.

With every joke, the past we tease,
In friendly jests, we find our ease.
Each chuckle shared is a treasure found,
In laughter's glow, our hearts unbound.

Hearts Aligned in Silence

In quiet moments, our souls embrace,
No need for words in this sacred space.
With every glance, we understand,
Two hearts aligned, a gentle hand.

In stillness, we share what's true,
An unspoken bond just me and you.
In the silence, love softly stirs,
A language of love that never slurs.

Solace in Union

In quiet moments, hands entwined,
Hearts whisper softly, paths aligned.
The world outside fades into night,
In your embrace, I find my light.

Through every storm, we stand as one,
Two souls together, fears undone.
With every breath, we forge our way,
In love's embrace, we choose to stay.

Reflections in a Shared Pool

Glimmers dance on waters still,
Echoes stir with gentle thrill.
In ripples deep, our stories weave,
Finding parts of us, we believe.

With each drop, a moment held,
In this pool, our secrets dwelled.
Together we flash, together we fade,
In reflections, our trust is made.

A Tidal Wave of Laughter

Laughter bursts like waves at sea,
Each sound a spark, wild and free.
Rolling on, it sweeps us near,
In shared joy, we have no fear.

Through playful jests, our spirits soar,
With every giggle, we ask for more.
In this tide, our worries erase,
Together we find our joyful place.

Still Waters

In calmness lies our secret space,
Where silence sings and hearts embrace.
The world outside may rush and roar,
But here, in stillness, we're restored.

Each glance a promise, each sigh a prayer,
In tranquil depths, we find what's rare.
With every heartbeat, we align,
In quietly woven threads, we shine.

Deep Connections

Beneath the surface, currents flow,
In hidden depths, true feelings grow.
With every glance, a story told,
In layers rich, we break the mold.

Bound by threads of shared delight,
Our souls entwined, igniting light.
In this embrace, we rise above,
Deep connections, endless love.

The Tapestry of Us

Threads of laughter weave through time,
Moments stitched with love so prime.
Colors bright in every hue,
A tapestry made just for two.

We dance beneath the stars so wide,
With dreams that swell like ocean tide.
Each pattern holds a tale untold,
Together, we spin our lives of gold.

With every knot, our hearts entwined,
In every fabric, our souls aligned.
Through trials faced and joys embraced,
A masterpiece, our love interlaced.

In silken threads, our stories blend,
A journey shared that will not end.
With every weave, our spirits sing,
In this tapestry, we are everything.

Sheltering Embraces

In the arms where warmth surrounds,
A refuge found in heart's soft sounds.
With every hold, a world ignites,
Sheltering love through darkest nights.

Whispers shared beneath the moon,
In quiet moments, we find our tune.
A haven crafted by gentle touch,
Where time stands still, we need so much.

Each heartbeat echoes through the night,
In shelter's glow, everything feels right.
Together we face the storms outside,
In your embrace, I choose to hide.

A fortress built of trust and care,
In every hug, no need to wear.
For in this space, we come alive,
With sheltering arms, we thrive and strive.

Reflections in Familiar Eyes

In your gaze, I find my way,
A journey traced in shades of gray.
Reflections spark of days gone by,
In familiar eyes, I learn to fly.

Through laughter shared and tears we've wept,
A bond so deep, our promise kept.
With every glance, a story flows,
In quiet moments, our love grows.

Silhouettes of dreams yet to be,
In your eyes, I find the key.
A mirror to the soul's sweet tune,
In familiar eyes, I feel the bloom.

As seasons shift and change their guise,
Forever, I will seek your eyes.
In reflections bright, we see the past,
In love's embrace, a bond so vast.

Unwritten Stories of Us

In the silence where dreams reside,
Awaits the tale of you and I.
With pages blank, yet hearts so full,
Unwritten stories ready to pull.

Every moment, a wordless theme,
Ink of laughter, threads of dream.
In every glance, a plot unfolds,
Our saga richer than words told.

Through winding paths and twists of fate,
We write our lines, it's never late.
With spirits bold, we pen the night,
Unwritten stories taking flight.

Together, we blaze through the unknown,
In each heartbeat, love has grown.
The future calls with whispers sweet,
In unwritten tales, our dreams complete.

Bridges Over Lonely Waters

Silent streams beneath the moon,
Whispers of a timeless tune.
Footsteps tread on weathered planks,
As shadows dance in soft, cool ranks.

Reflections shimmer in the night,
Carrying dreams in silver light.
A bridge of hope, steadfast and true,
Connecting hearts, from me to you.

Underneath, the currents flow,
Secrets hidden down below.
Yet here we stand, hand in hand,
On this bridge, together we band.

The lonely waters call our name,
Yet together, we'll stake our claim.
In each wave, a story's told,
Of passions whispered, brave and bold.

And when the dawn begins to break,
We'll cherish every step we take.
These bridges built on love's own flow,
Will guide us where we long to go.

Unspoken Understandings

In silence, we create our space,
A gentle smile, a soft embrace.
No words are needed, hearts align,
In quiet moments, love will shine.

The air is thick with what's not said,
In every glance, the truth is fed.
Connections grow without a sound,
In this still world, our dreams are found.

Shared laughter lightens heavy weight,
An unvoiced bond we cultivate.
Trust builds in every lived-out day,
In each small act, we find our way.

The rhythm of our hearts, a song,
In unison, where we belong.
No need for talk when souls can see,
The beauty in our harmony.

Together, we shall walk this line,
Unspoken ties, forever divine.
In every pause, a thousand themes,
Our hearts entwined, a life of dreams.

Interwoven Journeys

Paths converge under sprawling skies,
Where dreams are stitched in twinkling ties.
Each step we take, the fabric grows,
A story woven, life bestows.

Threads of gold and shades of gray,
Intertwined in the light of day.
Through trials faced and joys embraced,
A tapestry of time interlaced.

Diverging trails, then course aligned,
In every journey, love we find.
Through valleys low and mountains steep,
We carry on, our promise deep.

Every twist and turn we make,
Strengthens bonds that none can break.
In the grand design, we learn to see,
Our journeys blend in unity.

Together we will weave and flow,
A narrative only we can know.
In this wide world, hand in hand,
Our interwoven lives will stand.

Melodies of Coexistence

In harmony, the echoes play,
A vibrant dance in bright array.
Each note a thread, entwined and free,
In melodies of you and me.

Beneath the stars, the music swells,
A serenade of unseen spells.
In every chord, a shared glance grows,
Together in the notes, we chose.

Soft whispers ride on winds unleashed,\nIn every heart, the longing's reached.
Our lives compose a gentle song,
In resonance, where we belong.

With every swing, the world will sway,
In vibrant hues, we find our way.
Through harmonies, our spirits rise,
In coexistence, love never dies.

As rhythms pulse and feelings blend,
The harmony we craft won't end.
Together we'll create the sound,
In melodies profound, we're found.

A Cartography of Connection

In whispered paths we tread anew,
Mapping love in shades of blue.
With every step, two souls entwine,
Charting dreams, your heart in mine.

Lines of fate stretch far and wide,
In this journey, we confide.
Markers placed on maps we draw,
In connection's beauty, we find awe.

Beneath the stars, we sketch our way,
Each moment fleeting, none to stay.
Yet in this dance of hearts aligned,
A cartography is what we find.

Time bends as laughter paints the night,
With every glance, our spirits light.
Together in this vivid scheme,
We forge a love that's more than dream.

As seasons shift, the paths may change,
But in our bond, we never stray.
With every line and curve we trace,
A map of us in boundless space.

Echo Chamber of Hearts

In the silence, echoes grow,
Whispers soft, the truths we know.
In chambers deep where feelings bloom,
Resonance fills the empty room.

Each heartbeat calls, a gentle sound,
In rhythmic pulse, our love is found.
Reflections shine on polished walls,
In this space, our spirit calls.

Like ripples spread across still lakes,
The warmth of love, no heart forsakes.
In every sigh, a soft reply,
Together here, we soar and fly.

With every laugh, the walls vibrate,
In joy and pain, we contemplate.
An echo chamber forged in trust,
Where words and feelings blend, we must.

As shadows dance in golden light,
We find the strength to face the night.
In every echo, we reclaim,
The sacredness of love's sweet name.

Companions in Bloom

In gardens where our laughter grows,
Together tend to love's bright rose.
With gentle hands, we prune and care,
For every petal, a token rare.

Side by side, we watch dreams sprout,
In vibrant colors, there's no doubt.
With roots entwined in rich soil deep,
Companions in bloom, our secrets keep.

Seasons change, yet we remain,
Through summer's sun and autumn's rain.
Together facing winter's chill,
In every storm, we find our will.

In fragrant fields where memories weave,
We gather moments, hearts believe.
In petals soft, our stories blend,
As companions true, until the end.

When blossoms fade, we hold them near,
The beauty shared is crystal clear.
In every bud, our love will thrive,
Through every season, we are alive.

Threads of Our Stories

In tapestry of hearts we weave,
Each thread a tale we dare believe.
With colors bright, and shadows deep,
In every stitch, our secrets keep.

From distant lands to dreams up high,
Our stories flow like rivers nigh.
Connected yarn of past and now,
In woven paths, we take a bow.

As time unfolds, new threads emerge,
In harmony, our voices surge.
With laughter loud and whispers sweet,
Thread by thread, our lives complete.

In moments shared, the fabric grows,
With every laugh, a bond bestows.
In joys we find and sorrows share,
A story written, love laid bare.

Through life's loom, we stitch and bind,
Creating tales that intertwine.
In gentle hands, our stories thread,
Together, forever, hearts widespread.

Conversations Between Souls

In whispers soft, we find our way,
Two spirits dance, in night and day.
Thoughts entwined, like ivy's climb,
Echoes linger, across the time.

In silent stares, a world unfolds,
Stories shared, and secrets told.
Through laughter's light, and sorrow's shade,
Connections deep, that never fade.

With every word, a bond we weave,
In depths of trust, we truly believe.
Hearts aligned, in gentle sync,
In this moment, we find our link.

A gaze exchanged, a truth perceived,
In every breath, more is received.
The dance continues, a sacred rite,
Two souls entwined, in endless night.

In conversations, worlds collide,
With open hearts, we turn the tide.
Together we journey, hand in hand,
In this realm, forever we stand.

Canvas of Companionship

Brush strokes blend on life's vast sheet,
Colors mingling, a vibrant feat.
With every hue, our lives are shared,
In strokes of love, we're always paired.

Each canvas holds a tale untold,
Of dreams and hopes, in shades of gold.
We paint the skies, we shape the ground,
In every moment, joy is found.

Through laughter's hues and tear's clear blue,
We fill our canvas, me and you.
In every line, our stories dance,
In perfect rhythm, our souls' romance.

With open hearts, we share the brush,
Creating masterpieces in a rush.
In every layer, our lives reflect,
The bond we've forged, we won't neglect.

A canvas forged through thick and thin,
In every shade, our lives begin.
A masterpiece no eye can see,
But in our hearts, it will always be.

Weaving Lives Together

In threads of gold, our stories blend,
Each fiber strong, as we transcend.
With gentle hands, we craft our fate,
In woven patterns, we create.

Through trials faced, and triumphs sweet,
In every knot, a friendship meets.
Together we pull, we twist, we tie,
In this tapestry, you and I.

Colors vibrant, yet soft and true,
Every strand tells a tale of you.
In harmony, our hearts align,
In woven dreams, our souls entwine.

Through every turn, the loom we run,
The fabric speaks of all we've done.
In layers rich, our lives assert,
A legacy that will not hurt.

So let us weave, with love and care,
In this great quilt, a life we share.
United in thread, forever whole,
Together we rise, body and soul.

Windows to Shared Dreams

Through glass so clear, we gaze beyond,
Into the realms, where dreams correspond.
With open hearts, we seek to find,
A world of wonders, intertwined.

Each window frames a moment's grace,
Reflections dance, as fears embrace.
In visions shared, we soar and glide,
In colors bright, our hopes abide.

With each soft whisper, dreams unite,
In tranquil nights and morning light.
In visions cast, our journeys merge,
Through these windows, our souls surge.

As time unfolds, new dreams in sight,
Together we chase the stars so bright.
In every glance, a story starts,
A canvas painted by our hearts.

So let us peer, through each glass pane,
In unity, we'll break the chain.
A partnership, where dreams reside,
Windows open, side by side.

Conversations that Blossom

In quiet parks where whispers flow,
Two souls meet, with hearts aglow.
They share their hopes beneath the trees,
Like petals dancing in the breeze.

Laughter rings like chimes on air,
Every glance a brush of care.
Words weave tales of dreams untold,
A garden rich, in colors bold.

Through seasons change, they nurture trust,
In each exchange, discover lust.
For every word that softly blooms,
There lies a bond that brightly looms.

With every laugh, with every sigh,
In tender moments, spirits fly.
Conversations sprout like springtime flowers,
A testament to shared hours.

Beneath the sun, with shadows cast,
They jot their memories, hold them fast.
In every pause, a story grows,
In silent spaces, friendship flows.

A Canvas of Common Dreams

Two minds converge on an endless sheet,
Colors swirl, in rhythm, they meet.
A palette rich with hopes and fears,
Strokes of laughter and a few tears.

Each vision shared becomes a theme,
Creating splendor, a vivid dream.
With every hue, they sketch their plight,
In dusk's embrace, they find the light.

As shadows shift and shapes expand,
They trace together, hand in hand.
Through every line and every shade,
A world unfolds, where dreams cascade.

They blend their stories, hearts aligned,
In colors deep, their souls entwined.
As canvases catch the morning glow,
The beauty shines in what they know.

With brush in hand, they dare to soar,
Crafting futures on this lore.
In shared strokes, the truth ignites,
A canvas bright, reflecting lights.

Shared Paths through Time

Two travelers walking side by side,
Through winding roads, a gentle guide.
In laughter's echo, memories gleam,
Tracing footsteps, a shared dream.

The moments pause, yet never break,
Each landmark whispers, paths they take.
From silent woods to bustling streets,
Their bond strengthens in time's retreats.

With every mile, a story told,
In warmth of friendship, hearts unfold.
From dusk till dawn, they move as one,
In shared pursuits, the journey's fun.

Through valleys low and mountains high,
The stars above can't deny.
In every challenge, hand in hand,
Together strong, they make a stand.

For years will pass and seasons too,
Yet paths entwined will feel anew.
In memories forged, they always find,
A tapestry, beautifully entwined.

Unspoken Bonds

In silence shared, a glance will speak,
A language deep, though words are weak.
Between the lines, connection thrives,
In unvoiced thoughts, true love survives.

With every heartbeat, feelings grow,
A gentle warmth in twilight's glow.
No need for words, no grand display,
For in their hearts, they find their way.

A brush of hands, a fleeting touch,
In quiet moments, they feel so much.
In knowing smiles, they softly sway,
In unspoken bonds, they choose to stay.

With every sigh, a story weaves,
In stillness shared, the heart believes.
Through storms that roar and skies that clear,
Their bond remains, steadfast and near.

For in the depths of soul's embrace,
They find their home, a sacred space.
In silent love, together strong,
Unspoken bonds, where they belong.

Heartbeats in Synchrony

In quiet whispers, hearts align,
A dance of dreams, a bond divine.
Each pulse a promise, strong and true,
Together we stand, me and you.

Through stormy skies and sunny days,
Our rhythm flows in gentle waves.
With every beat, our spirits soar,
Forever linked, forevermore.

In shadows cast, in light we find,
The threads of fate that tie and bind.
With every heartbeat, love ignites,
Guiding us through the darkest nights.

So let this symphony unfold,
In every secret, every told.
In the melody of trust we share,
Our heartbeats dance, a perfect pair.

Together We Rise

Through trials faced, we stand as one,
No mountain high, no race to run.
With hands held tight, we feel the spark,
Together rising, brightening dark.

In laughter shared and sorrow's pain,
A bond unbroken, forever gained.
With every step, we climb the peaks,
A journey rich, in love it speaks.

Against the tides, we will not sway,
Together forging hope each day.
In unity, our voices strong,
Harmonies lift us, where we belong.

So here's to dreams, and skies so wide,
In this great dance, we will not hide.
With courage found, we aim to soar,
Together we rise, forevermore.

Madelines of Memory

In whispered tales of days gone by,
We find the threads that never die.
Each laugh, each tear, a sacred thread,
The madelines of all we've said.

Through dusty pages, time weaves slow,
Memories bloom, like flowers grow.
A taste of joy, a hint of tears,
In every slice, we face our fears.

Then gather 'round, let's share the feast,
Of laughter bright and love released.
For in each bite, our stories meld,
The sweetest truths, in hearts heldelled.

So lift a glass to what we've felt,
In every moment, love's been dealt.
Madelines soft, life's sweet embrace,
In memory's warmth, we find our place.

Rhythms of Friendship

In laughter shared, we find our beat,
A rhythm strong, a dance so sweet.
Through ups and downs, we move as one,
With every step, our hearts have spun.

In quiet moments, hand in hand,
We weave our tales, we make our stand.
With joy ignited, spirits sing,
In every glance, the joy we bring.

Together facing life's grand stage,
Our friendship writes a vibrant page.
With trust as strong as steel can be,
We face the world, just you and me.

So let us dance to friendship's tune,
Under the sun, beneath the moon.
In every heartbeat, every sigh,
The rhythms of friendship never die.

Intertwined Like Vines

In a garden where dreams entwine,
Two souls connected, like soft twine.
Under the sun, they gently climb,
Together they flourish, in perfect rhyme.

Whispers flow through leaves so green,
In the silence, their love is seen.
Like tendrils reaching for the light,
They hold each other, day and night.

Through storms and winds, they bend and sway,
Yet never break, they find their way.
Roots so deep, in soil they trust,
In every challenge, they adjust.

With every season, they grow anew,
Painting the sky in shades of blue.
Each moment shared, a fragrant bloom,
Their hearts entwined, dispelling gloom.

In the tapestry of life, they thrive,
Two vines together, forever alive.
With love as their anchor, they will find,
A journey sweet, intertwined like vines.

Boughs of Friendship

Underneath the towering trees,
Where laughter dances with the breeze.
Boughs of friendship stretch so wide,
In their shade, we joyfully bide.

Moments shared like sunlight's glow,
In every season, our bond will grow.
Through laughter, tears, and whispered dreams,
Together we are, or so it seems.

Branches twined, we weather storms,
In every shape, our love transforms.
With roots so strong, we stand our ground,
In the hush of night, our hearts resound.

When shadows fall and darkness creeps,
In your embrace, my spirit leaps.
With every step, through thick and thin,
In boughs of friendship, we begin.

So here's to us, as seasons change,
In harmony, our lives arrange.
With laughter echoing through the years,
Boughs of friendship calms our fears.

A Symphony in Two Keys

In a hall where echoes meet,
Two melodies compose their feat.
One in major, bright and fair,
The other soft, like whispers rare.

Together they dance through harmony,
An opus born of you and me.
With every note, a story's spun,
In this duet, we become one.

The strings strum sweet, the chords align,
In every measure, our hearts entwine.
Pulsing rhythms, a tender embrace,
In music's arms, we find our place.

Through crescendos, our spirits soar,
In this symphony, we crave more.
Contrasting shades, yet lost in bliss,
In harmony's grip, we find our kiss.

So let the world play on outside,
In this duet, forever abide.
With every heartbeat, the magic reveals,
A symphony in two keys, our love seals.

Rituals of Togetherness

In the warmth of shared laughter,
Hearts beat with the same drum,
Hands entwined, we gather closer,
In moments where we all come.

Candles flicker in a circle,
Whispers dance upon the air,
Each word a precious token,
A bond too precious to bear.

As the sun dips into twilight,
We give thanks for what we've shared,
Underneath the fading daylight,
Our spirits rise, unprepared.

In the silence, hands are clasped,
Promises made, anew to keep,
In this space, our hearts enrapt,
A love that's deep, a love that's steep.

When we part at dawn's first light,
Carry these moments, so divine,
Together we create our flight,
In memories, our souls align.

Voices in Perfect Harmony

Notes entwine like woven threads,
Melodies soar, sweet and bright,
In unison, our song spreads,
Filling the void with pure delight.

With every rise and every fall,
Voices blend in perfect tune,
Echoes dance within the hall,
A symphony beneath the moon.

Days may fade and seasons change,
Yet our chorus shall remain,
In the beauty, we are strange,
Yet together, we sustain.

Through the struggles and the cheer,
We find strength in every note,
With each lyric, we draw near,
In our heartbeats, there's a vote.

When silence falls, our souls still sing,
A harmony that never breaks,
In the love that joy will bring,
Together, make no mistakes.

Neon Dreams Under Stars

City lights flicker like fireflies,
Neon colors splash the night,
Underneath the cosmic skies,
We chase dreams that feel so right.

With laughter shared on bustling streets,
Footsteps echo with the beat,
In the rhythm of our heartbeats,
Together, we can't be beat.

Every glance a spark ignites,
Adventures waiting to unfold,
Hand in hand, we scale the heights,
Embracing all the brave and bold.

Lost in moments, time stands still,
Underneath the sparkling lights,
With each whisper, we fulfill,
The neon dreams that reach new heights.

Upon the rooftops, side by side,
The stars wink down with soft regard,
In this chaos, we abide,
In every dream, we find our yard.

Kaleidoscope of Kindred Spirits

In each other's eyes, we discover,
A world of light and colors bright,
Reflecting the warmth of a mother,
In laughter, we find our delight.

Every heart a unique shade,
Blending in a vibrant view,
In the bonds we carefully laid,
Our truths reveal what's pure and true.

Together we paint our stories,
With strokes of joy, fear, and grace,
A canvas bursting with glories,
A safe and accepting space.

As time whirls in a dance,
We embrace the ebb and flow,
In the currents, take a chance,
In our unity, we grow.

With every twist, our spirits gleam,
In the kaleidoscope of days,
We exist, a shared dream,
In this beautiful, complex maze.

Guiding Stars of Affection

In twilight's calm embrace we stand,
The stars above, a gentle band.
Each twinkle whispers love's sweet song,
In their soft glow, we both belong.

Through night's curtain, warmth is found,
In silent bonds that weave around.
A spark ignites, our spirits soar,
Guiding stars, forevermore.

With every wish upon a light,
We forge our dreams, igniting night.
Together chasing cosmic streams,
A dance of hope, a tapestry of dreams.

No shadows cast upon our path,
United hearts, we find our math.
In the universe, we claim our place,
Each heartbeat echoes, purest grace.

So let the cosmos weave our fate,
As stars align, it won't be late.
In genuine love, our spirits blend,
(Everlasting) no need to pretend.

Echoes of Kindred Spirits

Among the whispers in the air,
Our souls connect, beyond compare.
Voices soft like autumn leaves,
In harmony, the heart believes.

With every laugh, a thread is spun,
Memories dance, they're never done.
A melody of shared delight,
Echoes linger into the night.

Through trials faced, we stand as one,
A kindred dance, two hearts undone.
In silent moments, words collide,
The strength of love is our guide.

Like rivers flowing side by side,
In every tide, our hopes abide.
Together facing storms and fears,
Kindred souls, through all the years.

And when the night seems vast and long,
Our spirits sing a vibrant song.
In echoes loud, we find our voice,
With every breath, we make our choice.

The Dance of Familiar Hearts

In gentle steps, we sway and glide,
Two familiar hearts, side by side.
The rhythm builds, it pulls us near,
With every beat, the world disappears.

Twilight's shimmer casts a glow,
As shadows blend with what we know.
A dance of grace, a fluid flow,
In this embrace, love starts to grow.

Around us, whispers start to fade,
In spotlight's glow, our fears are laid.
A tapestry of dreams unfurled,
Together, we create our world.

With every twirl, our souls entwine,
In this ballet, our spirits shine.
A perfect waltz in harmony,
Two hearts in sync, so wild and free.

And as the night begins to close,
The dance remains in twilight's prose.
Familiar hearts, forever true,
In every step, I find my cue.

A Journey Shared in Silence

Through silent woods, we softly tread,
In quiet thoughts, our hearts are fed.
No need for words, the stillness speaks,
In every glance, our spirit seeks.

Beneath the trees, life gently flows,
In tranquil peace, the journey grows.
With every step, the world stands still,
In silence shared, we find our will.

The rustling leaves, a soft refrain,
In calm surroundings, we feel no pain.
Together lost, yet found anew,
In tranquil moments, just us two.

Through winding paths and hidden trails,
Our hearts are sails against the gales.
Each heartbeat synchronized in grace,
In the quiet, love finds its place.

So here we walk, hand in hand,
In shared silence, we understand.
A journey long, yet ever near,
In every breath, your essence clear.

Choreography of Friendship

In laughter's dance, we glide and sway,
With open hearts, we find our way.
Through every step, we share the sound,
In unity, our joys abound.

We twirl through hours, both near and far,
A bond unbroken, like a star.
In whispered secrets, trust is spun,
Our choreography, two as one.

When storm clouds gather, strong we stand,
With steady rhythm, hand in hand.
In imperfect moves, we learn to thrive,
Together, always, we come alive.

Every stumble's met with grace and cheer,
You lift me up when shadows near.
The music swells, a timeless tune,
In friendship's dance, we chase the moon.

With every heartbeat, we create the song,
A melody of love, where we belong.
So here's to us, the steps we take,
In this grand dance, our spirits wake.

Beneath the Same Sky

Under the vast and endless blue,
We share our dreams, both old and new.
With every dawn, a fresh delight,
Together we stand, hearts ignited bright.

The stars align while we hold tight,
Whispered hopes in the still of night.
One world, one path, though far apart,
Beneath the same sky, we share one heart.

When shadows fall, and fears take flight,
You light the way, a guiding light.
Through winds of change, we hold our ground,
In every heartbeat, love is found.

Together we dream, and together we fly,
Connected forever, you and I.
In every sunset, we see the grace,
Beneath the same sky, our rightful place.

As seasons change, our bond remains,
Through sunlit joys and gentle rains.
In every tear, in every smile,
Beneath the same sky, we walk the miles.

Love's Gentle Embrace

In quiet moments, soft and sweet,
Love wraps around us, a tender sheet.
With every glance, a story told,
In warmth, we find our hearts unfold.

Through woven whispers, secrets shared,
In love's embrace, we are prepared.
The world may spin, but we stand still,
With open hearts, we bend to will.

A gentle touch, a soft caress,
In love's embrace, we find our rest.
Through trials faced and fears we chase,
Our souls entwined in time and space.

When storms arise and shadows loom,
Your love's a light that dispels the gloom.
In laughter's echo, in silence deep,
In love's embrace, our promise to keep.

Two hearts together, forever entwined,
In love's embrace, joy we find.
In every moment, let love expand,
Together, forever, hand in hand.

Shadows Cast by Shared Light

Together we stand, in shadows so bright,
Illuminated paths in the heart of the night.
With every laugh, and every tear,
In shared light, we have nothing to fear.

Creating memories, both old and new,
In moments cherished, our spirits grew.
While shadows may dance, and time may flee,
Our light stays strong, you shine with me.

In the quiet whispers, a bond we trace,
Casting shadows, yet finding grace.
Through trials faced, our spirits rise,
With shared light, we touch the skies.

Through every challenge, together we stride,
With courage and love, we take it in stride.
In the glow of hope, shadows retract,
In our shared light, there's nothing we lack.

So here's to the moments, forever we weave,
In shadows cast, it's love we believe.
With every heartbeat, our journey's song,
In shared light, together we're strong.

Symphony of Hearts Aligned

In harmony we stand, side by side,
Melodies of dreams and hopes collide.
Every heartbeat sings a vibrant tune,
A symphony beneath the silver moon.

Each note a whisper, soft and tender,
Together we rise, love a warm contender.
In this dance of souls, we intertwine,
A cherished bond, forever divine.

Through trials faced and shadows cast,
Our unified pledge, destined to last.
In laughter shared, in tears we find,
The rhythm of hearts, beautifully aligned.

With each sunrise, a fresh refrain,
Our hearts compose through joy and pain.
In the silence, we find our song,
A harmony where we both belong.

Let the world listen, let it see,
The power of love, wild and free.
In every heartbeat, a story to tell,
In this symphony where we both dwell.

Bridges Built in Silence

In quiet moments, we find our way,
Through unspoken words that softly sway.
A glance, a nod, in the still of the night,
Building bridges from shadow to light.

Each silence a step, a path we tread,
With every heartbeat, our spirits spread.
The strength of trust in the space between,
Crafting connections, serene and unseen.

Through storms we've weathered, hand in hand,
These bridges rise, strong and grand.
In whispers of hope, in unvoiced dreams,
We find our strength, or so it seems.

Let the world around us fiercely roar,
In our quietude, we seek much more.
In the silence, love's foundation grows,
A testament to the bond that flows.

Together we stand, no words need be said,
With hearts that synchronize, gently led.
Through the stillness, we endlessly forge,
Bridges of silence, an eternal gorge.

Mosaics of Mutual Understanding

In fragments of life, we piece together,
Colors and textures that only tether.
Each shard a story, of struggle and grace,
Creating mosaics in a shared space.

Every moment shared, every laugh and tear,
Paints a picture of wisdom, rich and clear.
In our differences, beauty unfolds,
Tales of truth that nobody holds.

With eyes wide open, we seek to see,
The depths of you, the heart of me.
In silence and speech, our spirits blend,
Crafting a canvas where hearts can mend.

Through trials and triumphs, hand in hand,
In this vibrant mosaic, we take a stand.
Together we carve an artistic spree,
A masterpiece born from you and me.

So here we gather, souls intertwined,
In the dance of understanding, brightly aligned.
A tapestry woven, vibrant and bold,
In this mosaic of life, our story's told.

Unity in Diversity

Among the shades of life's vast hue,
We find our strength in the unity of you.
Different paths, stories that weave,
A tapestry of hope for all to believe.

In every culture, a beauty shines,
Threads of kindness in countless lines.
Together we blossom, like gardens in bloom,
Embracing the light that can cut through the gloom.

In the symphony of voices, loud and soft,
We rise together, our spirits aloft.
With open hearts, we blend and share,
In this unity, the world becomes rare.

Every smile shared breaks down the wall,
In acceptance, we answer love's call.
The richness of life in our hands, we hold,
United in diversity, a story unfolds.

So let us stand, hand in hand, as one,
In the dance of our differences, much can be done.
For together we thrive in this grand expanse,
A beautiful world, a harmonious dance.

Joy in Mundane Moments

In the kitchen, morning light,
Coffee brews, a warm delight.
Birds chirp softly, day will start,
Simple joys, they warm the heart.

A walk outside, the breeze does play,
Leaves dance gently, come what may.
Children laugh in the park nearby,
Moments pass like clouds in sky.

Worn book pages, tales unfold,
Stories shared, both new and old.
Laughter echoes, fingers trace,
In this time, I find my place.

Baking cookies, scent divine,
Flour dust like snow does shine.
Friends gather, smiles abound,
In little things, joy is found.

Evenings spent, the stars emerge,
Softly glowing, thoughts converge.
In every moment, bliss does bloom,
In mundane, life's sweet perfume.

Stitched Together with Care

Threads of silver, colors bright,
Stitch by stitch, we weave the light.
Fabric tells our story true,
In every seam, a bond we grew.

Embroidered dreams, patterns blend,
Every patch, a love we send.
Hearts entwined in every fold,
Memories warm, like woven gold.

Fingers dance with needle swift,
Creating beauty, a precious gift.
Together, crafting each new day,
In threads of love, we find our way.

Each small knot a tale retold,
In fabric, our lives unfold.
Through every tear, every repair,
We are stitched together with care.

As seasons change, our quilt grows wide,
In patches bright, our hearts abide.
Together forever, side by side,
In love's embrace, we take our ride.

The Language of Shared Silence

In quiet moments, hearts align,
No need for words, your hand in mine.
Time stands still, the world fades out,
In silence deep, we dance about.

A glance exchanged, we understand,
A language felt, not spoken, planned.
In every breath, a story shared,
In the stillness, love declared.

Clouds drift slowly, shadows play,
In this calm, we find our way.
Softly lingering, thoughts entwined,
In silent whispers, peace we find.

The night envelops, stars aglow,
In this silence, feelings flow.
A world of dreams, with you I roam,
In shared silence, we feel at home.

Morning breaks, the light returns,
In the quiet, our passion burns.
Words may falter, but love stays strong,
In silent bonds, we both belong.

Footprints on Parallel Paths

Side by side, we walk this lane,
Footprints line the road, remain.
Though separate ways may often bend,
The bond we share will never end.

In laughter shared, in tears we cry,
Parallel paths beneath the sky.
Time may stretch, and distance grow,
Yet in our hearts, we'll always know.

Crossroads come, choices made,
Yet friendships strong, will never fade.
Through golden fields and highest hills,
Together, chasing hopes and thrills.

As seasons shift, and colors change,
Our dreams may look a little strange.
But in the journey, hand in hand,
Together still, we firmly stand.

So here's to paths, both wide and narrow,
To every joy, every sorrow.
In the tapestry of life, we find,
Footprints shared, two souls intertwined.

Unity in Symphony

In harmony we stand together,
Melodies weave through the air,
Voices blend like warm soft weather,
Creating music, bright and rare.

Each note holds a story deep,
Resonating heart to heart,
In this dance we find our keep,
Unity plays its vital part.

Hands unite, a rhythmic flow,
With every beat, we find our way,
In the lights, our spirits glow,
Together we shall seize the day.

Moments shared, both joy and strife,
In this symphony called life,
Together we shall write the score,
A masterpiece forevermore.

In laughter bright, the shadows fade,
With every chord, we rise anew,
A vibrant world of dreams we've made,
In unity, we shall break through.

Paintbrush of Memories

Moments captured on a canvas wide,
Colors blend like sweet embrace,
Every stroke, a tale inside,
Time stands still in this sacred space.

Brush in hand, we carve our path,
Every hue tells where we've been,
Gentle strokes that spark our laugh,
In the canvas, love is seen.

Shadows dance in golden light,
Whispers echo in the night,
Each color speaks of joys and fears,
A masterpiece of fleeting years.

Together painting, hand in hand,
Our memories, like stars, align,
Brushes dipped in life's command,
Creating stories, yours and mine.

A tapestry of laughter, tears,
In swirling shades of soft delight,
Our friendship brightens all our years,
United in this art of life.

Skylines of Togetherness

A skyline shaped by dreams we share,
Underneath the vast expanse,
We build our hopes with tender care,
In every glance, there lies a chance.

With every brick, a memory laid,
In laughter echoing through the night,
Our bonds unbreakable, never swayed,
A fortress built on love and light.

Through storms we'll learn to stand as one,
Guided by the stars above,
Together, we have just begun,
To thrive in this city of love.

The sun sets low, yet still we rise,
With every dawn, our spirits soar,
In unity, we'll claim the skies,
With dreams that stretch forevermore.

As skylines change, our hearts remain,
Anchored in this bond we weave,
Together through joy and through pain,
In togetherness, we believe.

Navigating Life's Currents

In rivers wide, we drift along,
With every wave, our fears subside,
Together, we are ever strong,
In currents deep, we shall abide.

With oars in hand, we steer our way,
Through storms and calm, we find our course,
In laughter's light, we choose to stay,
With friendship as our guiding force.

The tides may rise, yet we hold fast,
In harmony, our hearts will sing,
With every turn, our bond will last,
In this great sea, it's love we bring.

Each journey's bend, a lesson learned,
In every splash, a tale is spun,
With vibrant dreams and spirits burned,
Navigating till the day is done.

Through life's vast ocean, side by side,
In every crest, we make our mark,
Together in this endless ride,
We'll navigate, ignite our spark.

Tapestry of Us

In threads of joy, we weave our dreams,
Moments stitched in laughter's seams.
With colors bright, our stories blend,
A tapestry rich, where love won't end.

Through storms we faced, our bond holds tight,
In darkest days, you are my light.
Each golden thread, a memory spun,
Together as one, our journey begun.

With every heart, a tale to tell,
We share the burdens, lift each other well.
In every patch, a secret shared,
A tapestry crafted, for it's truly rare.

As seasons change, we laugh and grow,
In every wrinkle, our love will show.
A beautiful weave, like stars above,
In the fabric of life, forever love.

So let us cherish this work of art,
Each thread a promise from the heart.
In the tapestry of us, we'll ever stay,
Together woven, come what may.

Echoes of Companionship

In the silence, your laughter rings,
Carving joy as the heartstrings sing.
With every word, a bond is cast,
Echoes of love, so deep and vast.

Through crowded rooms, our souls align,
In glances shared, a spark divine.
Whispers soft, in shadows play,
Companionship blooms in bright array.

Together we wander, hand in hand,
In shared adventures, we understand.
Through laughter's call and sighs of woe,
In echoes of us, our spirits grow.

As twilight whispers, we find our place,
In every memory, time cannot erase.
With every heartbeat, the world grows clear,
In the echoes of love, you are always near.

So here we stand, two souls entwined,
In life's sweet symphony, forever aligned.
Let every echo tell our tale,
In companionship's grace, we shall prevail.

Dance of Souls Intertwined

In twilight's glow, we find our beat,
Two hearts in rhythm, a gentle feat.
With every step, our spirits soar,
In this dance of souls, we ask for more.

Through swirls of laughter, we spin around,
In the silence, our love is found.
With gentle grace, we move as one,
In the dance of life, our journey's begun.

Across the floor, our shadows sway,
In harmony's embrace, we lose our way.
With whispered dreams, we twine and bend,
In this sacred dance, there's no end.

In every twirl, our hearts do speak,
A melody sweet, gentle yet sleek.
Together we glide, through night and dawn,
In the dance of souls, we are reborn.

So let us waltz under the stars,
With dreams unfurling, no distance far.
In this dance of love, our paths align,
Souls intertwined, forever divine.

Light in Each Other's Eyes

In quiet moments, your gaze meets mine,
A spark ignites, a love so fine.
With every glance, the world fades out,
In light found in love, there's never doubt.

Through trials faced, we share the flame,
In the warmth of your heart, I feel the same.
With every whisper, we find our way,
In light's embrace, we choose to stay.

As dawn breaks through, your smile shines bright,
In the glow of your joy, everything feels right.
With twinkling eyes, the universe flows,
In light that we've shared, our true love grows.

In mirrored souls, reflections dance,
In the light of your love, I take a chance.
With every moment, hope is reborn,
In the light in your eyes, my heart is worn.

So let our love be a shining guide,
In the depths of night, we will abide.
For in the light that we share and see,
In each other's eyes, we're meant to be.

A Horizon Shared

A canvas wide beneath the sky,
Two souls meet, their spirits fly.
Colors blend in evening light,
Together they embrace the night.

With whispers soft that weave a thread,
They share their dreams, no words unsaid.
As stars arise, their hopes ignite,
They forge a bond, forever tight.

The waves may crash, the winds may change,
Yet through the storms, their hearts arrange.
With every dawn, new paths will prove,
That love endures, in every move.

Along the shore where shadows play,
Their laughter dances, night and day.
In every glance, a promise made,
A horizon shared, never to fade.

So hand in hand, they face the morn,
In gentle light, their souls reborn.
With every step, their futures blend,
In unity, their spirits mend.

Paths Woven with Love

In the tapestry of time they tread,
Paths woven with love, beautifully spread.
Through valleys low and mountains high,
Together they soar, together they fly.

With every step, their heartbeat syncs,
In silent vows, their trust never blinks.
Through storms of doubt, they find their way,
In the light of love, forever stay.

Each twist and turn, a story told,
Of cherished moments, both brave and bold.
With hands entwined, the journey's new,
Paths woven tight, as worlds imbue.

In laughter shared and tears that fall,
They rise together, they never stall.
No matter the trials, come what may,
Their woven paths forever sway.

In the warmth of dusk, they pause and see,
How love's embrace has set them free.
With hearts aligned, their dreams ignite,
Paths woven with love, forever bright.

Garden of Kindred Hearts

In a garden where kindred spirits bloom,
Amidst the petals, dispelling gloom.
Each flower holds a whispered prayer,
For bonds that flourish, beyond compare.

With gentle hands, they tend the soil,
Nurturing roots through love and toil.
In the sunlight's grace, their laughter grows,
A vibrant tapestry, beauty shows.

Amidst the thorns, their patience shines,
Through trials faced, their love defines.
As seasons change, they hold each claim,
In the garden's heart, they feel the same.

Together they weave a fragrant dream,
In the night's embrace, they softly gleam.
With every bloom, their spirits rise,
In this garden, love never dies.

With every dawn, new colors burst,
A sacred bond, forever immersed.
In the garden where kindred hearts meet,
Life's sweetest blessings, so pure and sweet.

Lanterns Illuminating the Way

In the dark of night, they light the path,
Lanterns flicker, dispelling wrath.
With hopeful glow, their warmth extends,
Guiding each heart as the journey bends.

Through winding roads and shadows long,
In unity, they sing their song.
With every step, the light they share,
Illuminates dreams beyond compare.

As stars align in the vast expanse,
They find their courage, take a chance.
Each flickering flame, a guiding star,
Reminds them of just how loved they are.

In moments of doubt, they find their way,
Lanterns glowing, come what may.
With whispered hopes, they reach the dawn,
Together as one, they carry on.

So hand in hand, through night and day,
Their lanterns bright, lighting the way.
In love's embrace, they trust and stay,
With every heartbeat, come what may.

Harmony in Shared Moments

In the glow of twilight's grace,
We gather, time held still.
Laughter dances, memories trace,
Each heartbeat echoes, a gentle thrill.

Beneath the stars, we find our song,
Voices blend in sweet symphony.
In this space, we all belong,
Together, we weave our tapestry.

A touch of hands, a knowing glance,
In silence, words need not flow.
In shared moments, we find our chance,
To cherish the love that continues to grow.

Seasons change, yet bonds remain,
Like rivers that carve the stone.
In joy and sorrow, through joy and pain,
Together, never alone.

As day turns night with gentle ease,
We wrap in warmth, side by side.
In harmony, we find our peace,
In shared moments, hearts open wide.

Threads of Connection

In the fabric of time, we are stitched,
Each moment a thread, vibrant and bright.
Through laughter and tears, we're enriched,
Weaving a tapestry, pure delight.

The paths we choose, a dance of fate,
Intersecting lines form patterns new.
In every glance, we celebrate,
The beauty found in me and you.

Voices that whisper through the night,
Echoes of love that softly glow.
In darkness, we shine, a guiding light,
Carried by love's infinite flow.

Distance may stretch, yet hearts align,
In moments shared, we find our way.
The threads that bind, so pure, divine,
Keep us close, no matter the sway.

With each new dawn, connections grow,
In laughter, in love, they intertwine.
A journey continued, we come to know,
In threads of connection, we always shine.

Whispers of Togetherness

In the quiet hush of morning's light,
We share a breath, a soft embrace.
Whispers of love take gentle flight,
In togetherness, we find our place.

The world outside may rush and race,
But here within, time bends and sways.
In every glance, a sacred space,
Where silence speaks in countless ways.

Stories woven of warmth and grace,
In laughter shared, our spirits soar.
In every smile, familiarity's trace,
With you, my heart forevermore.

Moments cherished, a treasure rare,
In simple joys, we come alive.
Through every storm, we will repair,
In whispers sweet, our souls survive.

As the day fades and shadows blend,
Together, we find solace true.
In whispers soft, love has no end,
In togetherness, it's me and you.

Embrace of Solitude and Company

In quiet corners, we find our breath,
A dance of silence, soft and clear.
In solitude, we face the depth,
Of inner worlds, our hearts draw near.

Yet company calls, a gentle pull,
In laughter shared, we lose our cares.
In togetherness, our spirits full,
With memories made, the joy declares.

The art of being, alone, yet near,
In simple moments, comfort thrives.
A balance struck, no need for fear,
For in both spaces, love survives.

Through whispers soft, we intertwine,
Embracing both the we and I.
In solitude, we sip the wine,
While company lifts our spirits high.

In this embrace, we find our way,
A blend of quiet, a rush of cheer.
In solitude's light, in shared display,
We celebrate both far and near.

Mornings Over Coffee

Steam rises softly, morning light,
The world awakens, feels just right.
Sips of warmth, laughter shared,
In this moment, we are paired.

Pour another cup, dreams unfold,
Stories exchanged, both new and old.
Each sip a comfort, a gentle pause,
Together we savor, for this is ours.

Outside, the city begins to wake,
A dance of life, a rhythmic quake.
But in this nook, time stands still,
Two souls connect, hearts feel the thrill.

The taste of sunshine, the blend of spice,
In laughter and silence, we find our vice.
Moments blend sweetly, day drifts away,
Mornings over coffee, in the light we stay.

As the day beckons, we raise our hands,
To a world unknown, with shifting sands.
But in memories brewed, we'll always find,
Mornings like this, forever entwined.

Two Voices, One Song

In the quiet shadows, whispers blend,
Two hearts in rhythm, they transcend.
Melodies weave through the open air,
A symphony built on love and care.

Harmony dances, feelings ignite,
Each word a spark, a shining light.
Together we write, our verses strong,
In every note, two voices belong.

Through storms and calm, through laughter, tears,
In every measure, we face our fears.
Notes echo softly, a cherished refrain,
The beauty of us, in joy and pain.

With every chord, our spirits rise,
A canvas painted in love's disguise.
The world may fade, but we stay true,
In this magic, I find you.

As seasons change, we hold on tight,
To the song that started one fateful night.
Two voices in unison, forever strong,
In life's grand ballet, we sing our song.

Portraits of Friendship

Captured in laughter, a moment in time,
Brush strokes of kindness, a rhythm, a rhyme.
Each smile a canvas, each tear a hue,
In portraits of friendship, we meet anew.

Through trials we've faced, we've walked side by side,
In the gallery of life, we take our stride.
Colors of joy, shadows of pain,
Together we flourish, like sun after rain.

Stories engraved in the lines of our face,
In the warmth of our bond, we find our place.
The frame may be worn, but the memories shine,
In portraits of friendship, forever divine.

As seasons shift, our canvases blend,
Life's masterpiece crafted, my truest friend.
Each stroke tells a tale, from start to the end,
Together we flourish, as spirits ascend.

So here's to the colors that life can bestow,
In the gallery of laughter, the love that we sow.
May our portraits hang high, a beautiful sight,
Friendship forever, a source of delight.

Beneath the Same Sky

Stars sprinkle softly, in the velvet night,
Two souls wander under the same light.
Whispers of dreams, carried on the breeze,
Together we gaze, hearts at ease.

Each sunset a promise, each dawn a chance,
In the rhythm of time, we share our dance.
Clouds may gather, but hope will remain,
Beneath the same sky, we weather the rain.

Through valleys of shadows, and mountains so high,
We lift each other, as birds learn to fly.
The vastness surrounds us, yet here we stand,
Bound by our spirits, hand in hand.

In the quiet moments, and the storms that roar,
We're woven together, forevermore.
Each star a reminder of dreams we chase,
Beneath the same sky, we find our place.

As dawn meets the dusk, our stories entwine,
Under the heavens, where love will shine.
Together we journey, our hearts open wide,
Beneath the same sky, with you by my side.

The Dance of Together

In the gentle twilight's glow,
We whirl like leaves on high,
With every step, our spirits flow,
As stars embrace the sky.

Hand in hand, we twine and spin,
A melody so sweet,
Each heartbeat echoes from within,
As time feels slow, complete.

Through laughter's waves and whispers low,
We move, a tide of grace,
In this warm embrace, we know,
Together, we find our place.

The music plays, the world falls still,
With every spin, we soar,
A dance that bends the iron will,
With love, we ask for more.

As shadows stretch and colors blend,
Two souls in sync, we glide,
Each moment lived, a story penned,
On this sweet, endless ride.

Silent Songs of Unity

In quiet corners of the mind,
Soft echoes play their tune,
A harmony in stillness find,
Beneath the watching moon.

Our hearts beat softly in the dark,
In whispers, secrets shared,
In every silence, there's a spark,
Of joys and pains declared.

With every glance, a story told,
In gentle eyes, we meet,
A tapestry of warmth unfolds,
As spirits intertwine, complete.

The silent songs we sing inside,
Create a bridge of trust,
In unity, we shall abide,
Together, strong and just.

So let us find our way through night,
With love as our guiding light,
In every silence, pure delight,
Together, hearts ignite.

Together, We Breathe

In the stillness, side by side,
We draw the air, embrace the dawn,
With every breath, a love, our guide,
In harmony, we carry on.

The world may whirl, but we stand strong,
In whispered words, we find our beat,
A rhythm deep, where we belong,
Together, life feels sweet.

Through storms that rage and skies that cry,
Our lungs expand, release the fear,
With open hearts, we touch the sky,
In every moment, you are near.

With gentle sighs, our souls align,
In every laugh, we share the space,
Together, we breathe, a love divine,
In this sacred place, we trace.

So hand in hand, we dare to dream,
In every inhaled hope, we grow,
Together, we carve our shared theme,
In breaths exchanged, our spirits flow.

A Vow of Companionship

In the quiet vows we weave,
Promises bright, like morning light,
Through every joy and stormy eve,
We stand as one, hearts alight.

With words unspoken, trust we build,
In small gestures, love is shown,
A gentle heart, forever filled,
Our bond, a sturdy stone.

Though trials harsh may come our way,
We'll weather all, side by side,
In laughter, tears, come what may,
Together, we shall abide.

Each moment shared, a gift we keep,
In memories soft, we find our grace,
A sacred promise, soft yet deep,
In every breath, in every space.

So here we stand, our hands entwined,
With every heartbeat, vows renew,
In this companionship, we find,
A love that's ever true.

The Space Between Us

In silence we sit, side by side,
Yet oceans apart, our hearts collide.
A whisper of dreams, soft as the breeze,
Yearning for moments, as time seems to freeze.

The stars we gaze at, light-years away,
Carry the hopes we dare not say.
With every glance, a story unfolds,
In the space between us, a bond that holds.

Though miles may stretch without a sound,
In the quiet, our souls are found.
A dance of shadows, a gentle embrace,
In the space between us, we find our place.

With every heartbeat, a tether near,
In the distance, I still feel you here.
The space may be vast, but love is alive,
In every thought, our spirits thrive.

So let us cherish this vast expanse,
For in our hearts, we'll always dance.
Though paths may vary, our dreams align,
In the space between us, love will shine.

Embracing Fleeting Time

Moments like sand slip through our hands,
We chase after time, with hopes and plans.
Each tick of the clock, a precious gem,
Reminds us to cherish the fleeting hem.

The laughter shared, the tears we cry,
Each fleeting moment, a sweet goodbye.
In memories rich, we find the gold,
Embracing the stories, together told.

Every sunrise brings a brand new start,
Time whispers softly to each heart.
In the dance of days, we lose and find,
Embracing fleeting time, two souls aligned.

Each second a treasure, a gift in disguise,
In the rush of life, we must realize.
Hold close the laughter, the warmth, the light,
In embracing fleeting time, love ignites.

So let us savor each heartbeat's song,
For in this fleeting world, we belong.
Together we journey, hand in hand,
Embracing fleeting time, like grains of sand.

Sunlight Through Shared Smiles

A smile between us blooms like spring,
Bringing warmth that the sun can bring.
In that fleeting moment, joy takes flight,
Sunlight through shared smiles, pure and bright.

With every laughter, shadows fade,
In the light of joy, our fears allayed.
A connection forged in warmth and cheer,
Sunlight through shared smiles, ever near.

From whispered secrets to open grins,
In the dance of light, our story begins.
Together we shine, like stars in the night,
Sunlight through shared smiles, a beautiful sight.

In the tapestry woven with threads of love,
We find our strength, as we rise above.
The glow of our spirits, a guiding star,
Sunlight through shared smiles, no matter how far.

So let us embrace this radiant glow,
For in every smile, our hearts overflow.
Each shared moment, a brilliant ray,
Sunlight through shared smiles, forever stay.

The Rhythm of Togetherness

In the rhythm of hearts that beat as one,
We find a melody, love's gentle run.
With every step, we dance in time,
The rhythm of togetherness, so sublime.

Through laughter and tears, the music plays,
A symphony woven in ordinary days.
In harmony's embrace, we weave our song,
The rhythm of togetherness, where we belong.

Each heartbeat a note in a vibrant score,
Together we rise, together we soar.
In the cadence of life, hand in hand,
The rhythm of togetherness, perfectly planned.

With every struggle, every grace,
We find the rhythm in each embrace.
United we stand, through thick and thin,
The rhythm of togetherness, where love begins.

So let us dance to our own sweet sound,
In the rhythm of life, our joy profound.
For together we flourish, together we grow,
The rhythm of togetherness, our hearts aglow.

Harmony in Unison

In the quiet of the night,
Voices blend in gentle light.
Every note a soothing balm,
Together we find our calm.

Hands entwined, we start to sway,
Melodies guide us on our way.
In this dance of hearts aligned,
A symphony that fate designed.

Rhythms pulse through every beat,
With each step, our souls entreat.
In the laughter and the tears,
Harmony conquers all our fears.

Nature sings a perfect tune,
Beneath the watchful silver moon.
In every thrum, we feel the grace,
United, we share this space.

Through all seasons, thick and thin,
In our hearts, the song begins.
With each breath, we softly sing,
In unison, our love takes wing.

Threads of Connection

Woven deep in life's embrace,
Connections form a sacred space.
Each thread tells a tale unique,
In every bond, there's strength we seek.

Silken strands of joy and care,
Intertwined, they flow and share.
Moments captured, memories spun,
A tapestry of hearts as one.

Through the trials and the dreams,
Life's fabric ripples, softly gleams.
In every color, every hue,
We find a path to guide us through.

Each encounter, like a stitch,
In this quilt, we find our niche.
Together in the ebb and flow,
The threads of life continue to grow.

In laughter shared, and tears we shed,
The love we weave will never end.
Forever holding, side by side,
In our connections, we take pride.

Embracing Shared Moments

In fleeting instances, we find,
Beauty wrapped in space and time.
Every glance, a whispered truth,
Embracing joys of distant youth.

The clock ticks softly in the air,
While treasured seconds lay us bare.
In the warmth of silent gaze,
Shared moments, like a gentle blaze.

Side by side, in quiet grace,
We carve our dreams in open space.
Each heartbeat echoes, wise and slow,
In these moments, love will grow.

The world spins on, a fleeting race,
Yet we linger, hearts in place.
With every smile, a spark ignites,
In shared moments, pure delight.

As the sun dips low and fades,
We find comfort in the shades.
With every memory, a thread we'll spin,
Embracing nurtured hearts within.

Whispers of Togetherness

In the stillness of the night,
Whispers float, soft and light.
Thoughts unspoken, hearts entwine,
In togetherness, love will shine.

Glimmers dance in quiet dreams,
Every shared look, bursting seams.
Through gentle sighs, we breathe as one,
In togetherness, we've just begun.

The world outside may drift apart,
Yet here, we guard a sacred heart.
Through trials faced and laughter shared,
In whispers soft, our souls are bared.

Candle flames flicker in the dark,
Each flickering hue, igniting spark.
In the warmth of our embrace,
Togetherness, a welcome place.

Every moment, pure and true,
We find our strength in all we do.
In the whispers, sweet and low,
Together, love continues to grow.

Interlaced Journeys

Two paths converge beneath the sky,
Shared laughter echoes, memories lie.
Footsteps entwined on winding roads,
In every moment, a story unfolds.

Mountains bow to the moonlit nights,
In silent whispers, our future writes.
Through every trial, through every cheer,
We find our way, with hearts sincere.

The rivers flow, as dreams take flight,
In the dance of shadows, we find our light.
Hand in hand, through storms we'll roam,
In each other's arms, we build a home.

Across the valleys, we sing our song,
In vibrant colors, we both belong.
The tapestry woven with threads of fate,
Every stitch a moment, never too late.

As horizons stretch to meet the dawn,
We take a step, as dreams are drawn.
Interlaced journeys, hearts laid bare,
In the vastness of life, we find our share.

Handwritten Letters of Solace

Ink spills softly on weathered pages,
Each word a story through fleeting stages.
In the quiet night, your voice I hear,
Through handwritten letters, you draw me near.

A whisper of hope in each gentle line,
In solitude's grasp, your strength becomes mine.
Every sentence a bond, a soothing embrace,
In the ink's quiet dance, I find my place.

Beneath faded stamps, emotions unfurl,
With a flick of the pen, you paint my world.
Through storms and shadows, your thoughts reside,
In each treasured letter, love won't hide.

A symphony written in heartfelt tones,
Each letter a journey, we're never alone.
In the margins, your laughter finds voice,
In the cadence of writing, our hearts rejoice.

As pages turn, the seasons do change,
Yet our letters stay steady, beautifully strange.
With every return, I find solace and peace,
In handwritten words, our love won't cease.

Gardens Grown Together

In the heart of spring, we plant our dreams,
With seeds of promise, in gentle gleams.
Hands in the soil, we nurture and tend,
In every bloom, a story to send.

Roses and daisies, colors entwined,
In this shared garden, love's roots aligned.
A tapestry woven of sun and of rain,
Through laughter and tears, we grow through the pain.

Butterflies dance in the warmth of the sun,
In our fragrant haven, we find joy and fun.
Each petal holds whispers of moments we share,
In the beauty of growth, we find we care.

As seasons evolve, the harvest arrives,
With fruits of our labor, our spirit thrives.
Together we gather the essence of life,
In gardens we've tended, free of strife.

And even in winter, when blooms fade away,
Our love's evergreen will forever stay.
In the roots of our hearts, we know it's true,
In gardens grown together, it's me and you.

Celestial Companion

Beneath the stars, our dreams collide,
A universe painted, with hearts open wide.
In silent whispers, galaxies speak,
As the night wraps us in its velvet seek.

With a moonlit path, we tread with grace,
In the dance of shadows, we find our place.
Comets brush past, igniting the sky,
As we share our secrets, you and I.

Constellations align, a cosmic embrace,
In the vastness of space, we leave a trace.
With every heartbeat, the universe sings,
As we navigate through what starlight brings.

A celestial bond, woven by fate,
With every twinkle, we celebrate.
In the fabric of time, our spirits roam free,
In the cosmos together, just you and me.

When dawn breaks forth, the stars disappear,
Yet in our hearts, their light stays near.
As we journey onward through time and through space,
You're my celestial companion, my resting place.